Quran Stories for Little Believers

THE STORY OF THE FLY

by

SANIYASNAIN KHAN

Goodword kidz

Helping you build a family of faith

2

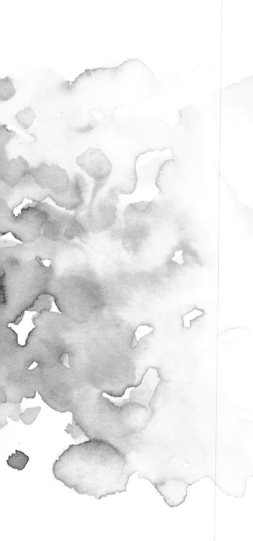

Have you ever
seen the little fly?

4

How it buzzes
around all the time,
and never gets
weary of its work?

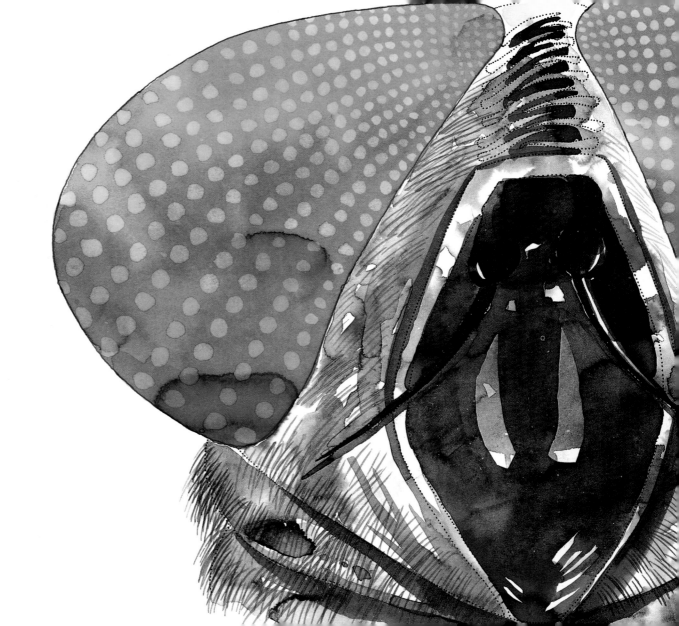

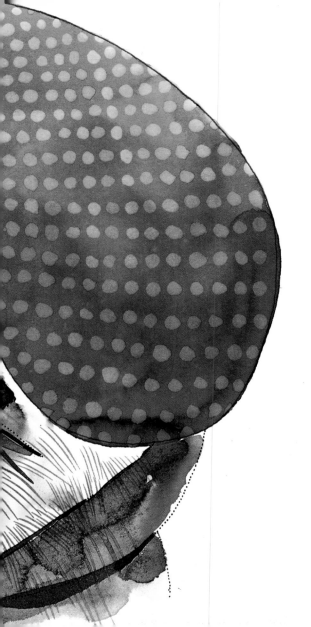

Did you know that the eye of a fly has thousands of lenses. Through these it can see behind it, so that no enemy can harm it.

The fly digests its food outside its body by pouring special liquid on it. Then it sucks in the digested food by absorbent pumps.

Only Allah could create
such an amazing creature.

Those who worship other gods should know that those they worship can never create even a single fly. Even if they all join together to do it.

13

More amazing
is that, if a fly
carried away a
speck of dust
from them, they
could never get
it back from it.

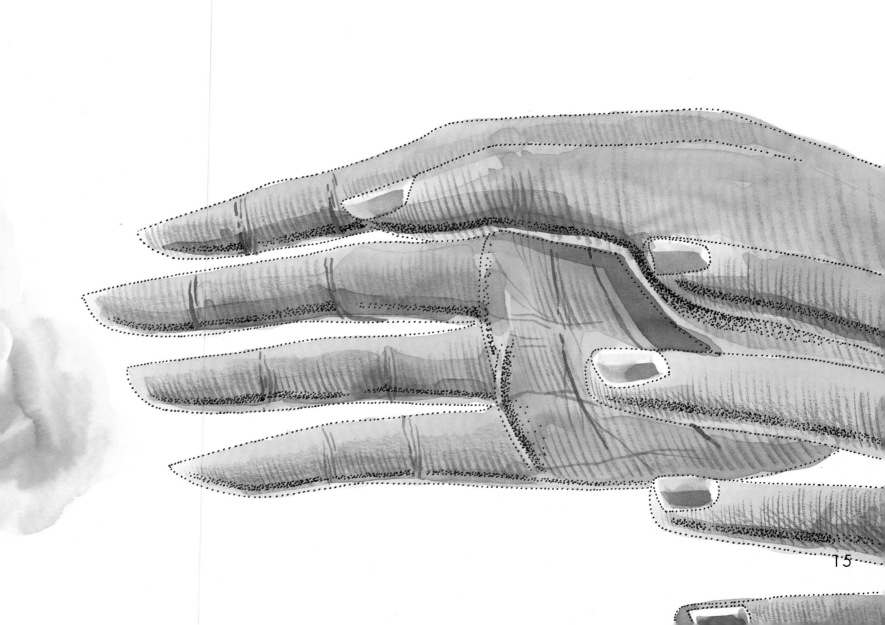

15

Thus let us worship Allah— the Creator of the heavens and the earth and all that exists between them.

Find out more, look up the following parts of the Quran: *Surah al-Hajj, 22:73.*